John A. Sundby

Johnny Sundby

[Front Cover Photo]

The Cathedral Spires, resembling European cathedrals, point to their maker in God's Country, the beautiful Black Hills. (John A. Sundby)

[Back Cover Photo]

Rose light rakes the relief of buttes in the Badlands. (Johnny Sundby)

Dedicated to:
Kathy and Bobby Sundby

Distributed by
RUSHMORE PHOTO & GIFTS INC.
3325 West Main Street
Rapid City, South Dakota 57702

Printed in Korea
For Terrell Publishing Company 0994197

PHOTOGRAPHY BY JOHNNY SUNDBY & JOHN A. SUNDBY
All rights to the photography are reserved by Johnny Sundby of Dakota Skies Photography
P.O. Box 8091
Rapid City, South Dakota 57709-8091

PHOTO CAPTIONS BY JILL SUNDBY

ISBN 1-56944-115-4

IN

GOD'S COUNTRY

A Collection of Photographs of the Black Hills & Badlands

BY JOHNNY SUNDBY & JOHN A. SUNDBY

THE remnants of an afternoon thunderstorm roll past the stark Badlands west of Cedar Pass Lodge.

THE waters that shroud these Spearfish Canyon walls were named for their likeness to a bride's veil, Bridal Veil Falls.

THE Eye of the Needle threads the evening sky.

T HE Black Hills soften to shades
of gray with each successive ridge.

JOHNNY SUNDBY

S YLVAN LAKE, actually a reservoir

constructed for a resort in 1891,

mirrors clouds on a summer day.

In the fall, Spearfish Canyon

displays its subtle splendor.

JOHN A. SUNDBY

THE setting sun burnishes Pactola Reservoir, named for the mining camp which once thrived at its bottom before the dam was finished in 1956 to hold water for the Rapid City area.

WHEAT ripens in amber waves of grain near the small town of Scenic.

Peaceful Rapid Creek turned
into a raging river on June 9,
1972, killing 238 people in and
around Rapid City.

John A. Sundby

Johnny Sundby

Spearfish Creek winds its way
through fall foliage in colorful
Spearfish Canyon.

THE last light of day touches
the tops of the Cathedral Spires
as viewed from the summit
of Harney Peak.

JOHNNY SUNDBY

JOHNNY SUNDBY

SOUTH DAKOTA'S state flower,
the pasque, blooms in early spring
throughout the Black Hills.

JOHNNY SUNDBY

MOVING clouds paint brush-
strokes across the midnight sky.

JOHN A. SUNDBY

I N the quiet of winter, snow dusts the serene Cathedral Spires.

JOHNNY SUNDBY

T HE bronze waters by the Pacto-la shoreline create a patterned tapestry at sunset.

JOHNNY SUNDBY

W*ATER* cascades over Roughlock Falls in Spearfish Canyon at Savoy.

JOHN A. SUNDBY

S*EDIMENT* from an ancient sea forms the limestone walls of Spearfish Canyon in this view from the Latchstring Village at Savoy.

DEVILS TOWER, in the north-western corner of the Black Hills, is believed by some geologists to be the core of an ancient underground volcano. It was the film site for the movie "Close Encounters of the Third Kind."

WILDFLOWERS in a myriad of hues bloom each summer in the Black Hills.

A boulder bathes in the mist of Roughlock Falls.

Aɴ Easter morning sunrise warms the South Dakota sky as viewed from Highway 16.

W INTER transforms Spearfish
Creek into a tranquil Christmas
card scene.

W IND CAVE is famous for its
boxwork, which forms when min-
erals crystallize in softer rock,
which later dissolves.

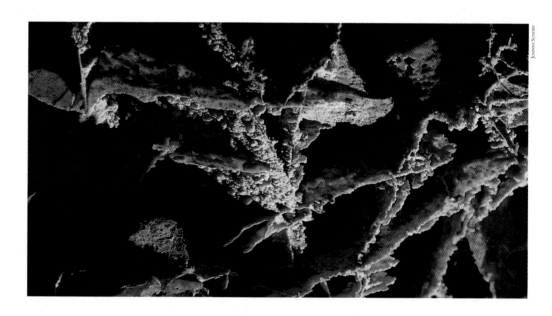

A splash of sunflowers paints the arid landscape of the Badlands west of Cedar Pass.

D̄EVILS TŌWER National Monument pierces a sapphire sky.

JOHNNY SUNDBY

A silken stream weaves through Spearfish Canyon.

JOHNNY SUNDBY

A lone rider returns home
after a last check over his herd
east of Rapid City.

JOHNNY SUNDBY

SPECTATORS enjoy a kaleidoscope of colors at the annual Elks Club Balloon Rally in Rapid City.

A ranger hangs on the stone eyelash of Thomas Jefferson on Mount Rushmore patching cracks. Each year, cracks are filled with a silicone building material to retard erosion.

JOHN A. SUNDBY

BEN BLACK ELK, was photographed by millions of Mount Rushmore visitors from the 1940's until his death in 1972. Ben was the grandson of Oglala Sioux holy man Black Elk.

JOHNNY SUNDBY

A horse and rider step gingerly into the frigid December waters in Dark Canyon west of Rapid City.

A hot air balloon drifts quietly above the Shrine of Democracy.

Johnny Sundby

COWBOYS on the Pine Ridge
Indian Reservation finish the
day's chores.

Johnny Sundby

Johnny Sundby

A young Lakota fancy dancer
becomes a swirl of colors at the
"Come Dance With Us" powwow
in Rapid City.

AFTER leaping from his horse,
a bulldogger wrestles a steer,
easily twice the cowboy's weight,
at the All-Indian Crazy Horse
Stampede Rodeo.

JOHNNY SUNDBY

TWO young Lakota brothers think about the upcoming competition as they await their chance to dance at a Central States Fair powwow in Rapid City.

TWO climbers counterweight each other as they descend a granite spire in the Needles.

YOUNG horseback riders splash through Box Elder Creek at the Nemo Guest Ranch.

BUNGEE JUMPERS place their trust in God and in a high-tech harness and cord system when freefalling over 10 stories.

A rock climber rappels off a granite spire near Mount Rushmore.

PRACTICAL ranch skills have evolved into the West's popular sport of rodeo. Today professional cowboys make a living winning money on the rodeo circuit.

A skier soars into an azure sky at Terry Peak Ski Area, one of two ski areas near Lead in the Northern Hills.

A young cowboy practices his roping skills at the South Dakota High School Finals Rodeo in Sturgis.

A Pine Ridge rancher surveys goings-on at a large ranch south of Interior.

AN ice climber rappels down frozen Bridal Veil Falls in Spearfish Canyon.

A Lakota Sioux man enjoys the company of relatives and friends during the weekend festivities at the Veterans Powwow at Pine Ridge village .

JOHNNY SUNDBY

Eᴀᴄʜ spring ranchers brand their calves to prevent cattle rustling.

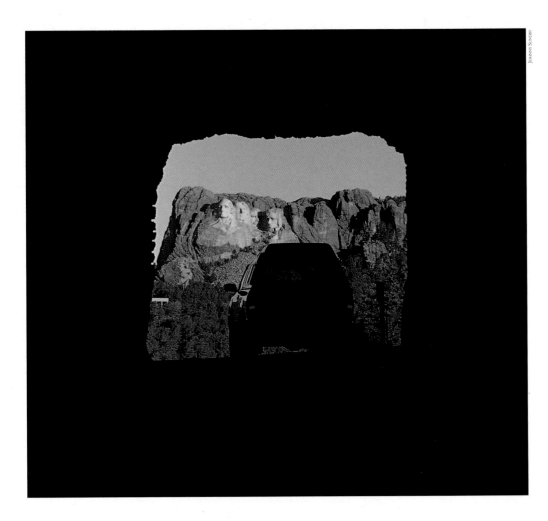

JOHNNY SUNDBY

Aᴛ tunnel on Iron Mountain Road frames the faces of Mount Rushmore.

JOHNNY SUNDBY

A climber rappels down the massive columns of Devils Tower. Since 1937, when records were first kept, over 28,000 climbers have scaled the 867 feet to its summit. The first ascent was in 1893.

JOHNNY SUNDBY

A snowboarder catches some "big air" off a cliff at Deer Mountain Ski Area.

SCULPTOR GUTZON BORGLUM
carved Mount Rushmore from
1927 until his death in 1941.
Each head is approximately
six stories tall.

JOHNNY SUNDBY

THE Badlands Loop Road snakes across the parched spine of Badlands National Park's western edge.

JOHN A. SUNDBY

Irises grow where children once played near a schoolhouse in the turn-of-the-century mining town of Spokane, located close to Iron Mountain Road. Numerous metals, including gold and silver, were mined there.

Open year-round, the Shrine of Democracy attracts over 2 million visitors annually.

JOHNNY SUNDBY

TAIL lights streak over Highway 244 behind Mount Rushmore at dusk.

JOHNNY SUNDBY

HOARFROST clings to an old wagon on a ranch near Rockerville.

WEEDS stretch toward a windmill near Hermosa.

BLACK HILLS climbers enjoy the vista from Tent Peg Spire in the Needles.

THE historic Finnish Church in Lead rests on blocks prior to being moved to accommodate the growth of Homestake's Open Cut mine.

BUILT on the Chicago, Burlington & Quincy Railroad line in 1889, this tall trestle between Custer and Hill City carried trains across the gorge for 94 years. In the mid 1970s, the 1880 Train crossed the bridge after flood waters washed out the Hill City to Keystone route.

AT 7,242 feet above sea level, Harney Peak is the highest peak east of the Rockies in the United States. The stone building on the summit was built by the Civilian Conservation Corps in 1938-39 and was a manned fire tower for over 30 years.

A<small>T</small> M<small>EMORIAL</small> L<small>AKE</small>, named for the victims who died in the 1972 Rapid City Flood, one's spirit can reflect along with the rising sun.

T<small>HE</small> faces of Mount Rushmore glow under a July moon during the lighting ceremony held each summer evening at the memorial.

RISING 1,200 feet above the prairie, Bear Butte is considered sacred by Native Americans who still come here to pray.

JOHN A. SUNDBY

CHANGING aspen trees line the narrow and twisting Iron Mountain Road near Keystone.

THE face of Thomas Jefferson was originally carved into the granite at George Washington's right. Due to unsuitable rock, the face was blasted off the mountain and carved to Washington's left.

NEEDLES Highway winds through granite spires, the core of an ancient Black Hills that once stretched nearly as high as the much younger Rockies.

T HE 5 a.m. sunrise illumi-
nates a grain elevator in Cotton-
wood as the full moon drops
into the horizon.

JOHNNY SUNDBY

QUAKING golden aspen leaves frame the faces of George Washington, Thomas Jefferson, Theodore Roosevelt, and Abraham Lincoln.

IN the southern Black Hills, Lakota leader Crazy Horse is emerging as the world's largest sculpture. Sculptor Korczak Ziolkowski (1908-1982) began the non-profit project at the invitation of Lakota chiefs.

A touch of cowboy humor is displayed in the worn boots that top fence posts along Highway 16 west of Custer.

IN any season, Mount Rushmore is spectacular. A unique side view is obtained by driving Highway 244 behind the memorial toward Hill City.

JOHN A. SUNDBY

JOHNNY SUNDBY

HISTORIC Deadwood, once home to Calamity Jane and Wild Bill Hickok, offers round-the-clock gambling, dining and dancing.

JOHNNY SUNDBY

WILDFLOWERS blanket a
field in front of a dilapidated
barn south of Lead.

JOHNNY SUNDBY

LIGHTNING cracks the night
sky over Rapid City.

A helicopter provides a dramatic panorama of the Badlands east entrance.

UNDER the midnight moon, dinosaurs still appear to rule the earth at Dinosaur Park in Rapid City.

JOHN A. SUNDBY

JOHNNY SUNDBY

Since their introduction into Custer State Park in 1924 from Canada, mountain goats have migrated and thrived in several areas of the Black Hills including the Mount Rushmore area.

A bison calf, less than one day old, takes its first steps on wobbly legs as its mother keeps a watchful eye.

Pronghorn antelope, which can reach speeds of up to 50 miles per hour, are the fastest land animals in North America.

Under a full moon, a bull elk

holds his ground on Boland Ridge

in Wind Cave National Park.

48

JOHNNY SUNDBY

JOHNNY SUNDBY

A bison bull forages his way up a gully in the Badlands where thousands of his ancestors once roamed before the arrival of the "wasichu" or white man.

ABOUT 40 turkeys roost in a leafless treetop near Hermosa dispelling the myth that turkeys cannot fly.

JOHNNY SUNDBY

BEAR cubs frolic at Bear Country U.S.A., one of several tourist attractions on Highway 16 south of Rapid City.

A large coil of rattlesnake sounds its warning with a nervous twitching of its tail.

JOHNNY SUNDBY

JOHNNY SUNDBY

Cᴜꜱᴛᴇʀ Sᴛᴀᴛᴇ Pᴀʀᴋ bison amble toward the park's buffalo corrals during the annual, fall roundup.

Sᴄʀᴇᴇᴄʜ ᴏᴡʟᴇᴛꜱ in a Rapid City park watch and wait for their mother to return.

JOHNNY SUNDBY

A bull elk bugles on a ridge at Wind Cave National Park at sunset during the fall rut.

Johnny Sundby

Hardier than cattle, Custer State Park bison rest while the snow falls.

Johnny Sundby

Hunters from many states come to western South Dakota each fall in search of trophies like this prize whitetail buck.

A young mare peeks shyly over her mother's back at the Black Hills Wild Horse Sanctuary, south of Hot Springs.

CURLED horns frame the face of a bighorn sheep resting in a meadow of wildflowers in Custer State Park.

IN the golden glow of first light, antelope graze on a grassy flat near Badlands National Park.

Johnny Sundby

Oɴᴄᴇ numbering in the millions, buffalo, or "tatanka" to the Sioux, supplied the plains Indians with food, clothing and shelter.

Johnny Sundby

Wɪʟᴅ ʜᴏʀsᴇs thunder across the grassy prairie of the Black Hills Wild Horse Sanctuary

ABOUT THE AUTHORS

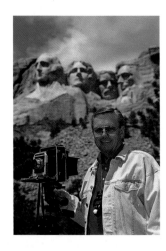

JOHNNY SUNDBY joined the photo staff of the *Rapid City Journal* in Rapid City, South Dakota, in 1991. He has also photographed for the *Associated Press* in Pierre, South Dakota, and with the *Miles City Star* in Miles City, Montana. His work has appeared in the *Associated Press, Baton Rouge Advocate, Boston Globe, Deadwood Magazine, Entrepreneur, Family Circle, Gamma Liaison, Indian Country Today, Lawyers' Weekly, Los Angeles Times, Ms., National Enquirer, Nation's Business, New York Times, Scholastic News, South Dakota Magazine, Sidney Morning Herald* and *USA Today.* Johnny is a graduate of Augustana College in Sioux Falls, South Dakota.

JOHN A. SUNDBY, a Realtor for the last 29 years, enjoys shooting large format photography as a hobby. Prior to selling real estate, he was a helicopter pilot and co-founder of the helicopter rides over Mount Rushmore which also provided him with a bird's eye view of much of Western South Dakota. His photo credits appear on numerous postcards of the Black Hills and especially Mount Rushmore, as well as several calendars, notecards, and the Rushmore commemorative stamp poster. John resides in Rapid City with his wife, Kathy. John is a graduate of St. Olaf College in Northfield, Minnesota.

JILL SUNDBY, caption writer and Johnny's sister, grew up in the Black Hills where exploring ghost towns occupied much of her time. As a writer, Jill interned with the *Rapid City Journal,* spent two years with the *Independent Record* in Helena, Montana, and five years with the *Billings* (Montana) *Gazette .* She authored *"Wagons Across Wyoming",* a photo-filled book on the Wyoming Centennial Wagon Train of 1990. Jill student taught on the Crow Indian Reservation in Montana before moving to Japan to teach English. She resides in Hokkaido, Japan, with her husband, Mark Van Alstyne. Jill is a graduate of St. Olaf College, and Montana State University in Billings.